Modern Miniatures for Piano Solo

Volume 2

Intermediate through Early Advanced

edited by Helen Marlais

THE FJH
CONTEMPORARY
KEYBOARD
EDITIONS

Dianne Goolkasian Rahbee

Production: Frank J. Hackinson
Production Coordinators: Philip Groeber and
                                          Isabel Otero Bowen
Cover: Terpstra Design, San Francisco
Cover Painting: Yellow, Red, Blue, 1925, W. Kandinsky
Engraving: Tempo Music Press, Inc.
Printer: Tempo Music Press, Inc.

ISBN-13: 978-1-56939-482-3

Copyright © MMV by
THE FJH MUSIC COMPANY INC. ASCAP
2525 Davie Road, Suite 360
Fort Lauderdale, FL 33317-7424
International Copyright Secured.
All Rights Reserved. Printed in U.S.A.

THE
F·J·H
MUSIC
COMPANY
INC.

Frank J. Hackinson

Notes from the Composer

These teaching pieces follow a long tradition of pedagogical works inspired by such composers as Czerny, Gurlitt, Heller, Burgmüller, Grieg, Tchaikovsky, Bartók, Kabalevsky, and others. They are written to challenge a student's mind, fingers, imagination, and soul.

Playing the piano has always been a great joy to me personally. The excitement of running my fingers over the keys in fascinating patterns of color and sound and exploring my imagination continues to give me immense pleasure. Developing a piano technique is disciplined brain and finger training similar to the kind necessary when one participates in an Olympic gymnastic sport; the more you practice, the better you become! I hope you enjoy these pieces. Perhaps you'll try composing some of your own.

Sincerely,
Dianne Goolkasian Rahbee

About the Composer

Dianne Goolkasian Rahbee, born in Somerville, Massachusetts, February 9, 1938, is a first generation Armenian-American whose father was a survivor of the genocide, and much of her music reflects a deep-rooted ethnic background. The strong influences of her first spoken language, Armenian, and of the folk music in the home where she grew up, are important elements in her musical language. Her early love for music was sparked by her mother, a talented violinist.

Dianne began her musical training as a pianist in Boston with Antoine Louis Moeldner, who studied with two of Leschetitzky's most illustrious pupils, Helen Hopekirk and Paderewski. The Moeldner-Hopekirk connection would have particular impact: Moeldner had been a teaching assistant to Ossip Gabrilovich, while Helen Hopekirk was herself a highly respected composer and pianist, and served as an early role model for Goolkasian Rahbee. The influence of this distinguished lineage was a powerful inspiration. She continued her studies at Juilliard as a piano major and at Mozarteum in Salzburg, Austria, studying chamber music with Enrico Mainardi. In later years, Dianne studied piano privately with David Saperton in New York and Lily Dumont, Russell Sherman, and Veronica Jochum in Boston. As a self-taught composer, she began writing pieces for her piano students and received encouragement to continue this work from Constance Keene and David Saperton among others.

At age 40, Goolkasian Rahbee began concentrating on composing, and has since produced a large body of works for piano solo, orchestra, instrumental ensembles, percussion, and voice. Her music is performed internationally, and many large festivals have featured her works in the U.S. and abroad.

A Special Note to Students

Welcome to the exciting world of music written for you during our time! The composer of this collection is someone you could actually speak to and meet! (If you would like to write to the composer of this book, send your letter to FJH and it will be given to her.) In this volume, you will discover new sounds and pedal effects, and interesting melodies, rhythms, and harmonies. You will notice that some of the pieces in this volume are programmatic lyrical gems, while others are a mixture of etudes for both study and performance. These studies are not only exciting to listen to and play, but they also help you grow as a pianist by concentrating on a single technical or musical feature while enjoying the piece. Some etudes stress intervals, scales, or arpeggios, while others focus purely on musical ideas.

As you explore this book, use your imagination to create your very own interpretation of these wonderful new pieces. The title of each work will give you your first clue as to how to bring the piece to life, and the musical indications (tempo, dynamics, articulation and pedal markings, etc.) will provide a map to guide you through this exciting musical journey.

Enjoy these pieces!

Sincerely,
Helen Marlais

About the Editor

Helen Marlais has given collaborative recitals throughout the U.S. and in Canada, Germany, Turkey, Hungary, Italy, Lithuania, Russia, and China. She is recorded on Gasparo and Centaur record labels, and has performed and given workshops at local, state and national music teachers' conventions, including the National Conference on Keyboard Pedagogy and the National Music Teacher's convention. She is Director of Keyboard Publications for the FJH Music Company and her articles can be read in major keyboard journals.

Dr. Marlais is an associate professor of piano at Grand Valley State University in Grand Rapids, MI. She has also held full-time faculty piano positions at the Crane School of Music, S.U.N.Y. at Potsdam, Iowa State University, and Gustavus Adolphus College.

4

Table of Contents
(Arranged in order of difficulty)

The intermediate level pieces are found on pages 6 through 27.
The late intermediate pieces are found from pages 28-57, and pages 66-68.
The early advanced pieces are found on pages 58-65, and pages 69 to the end.

Floating in Space
(Study in Perfect Fourths)
from Expressions
Op. 8, No. 6

Dianne Goolkasian Rahbee

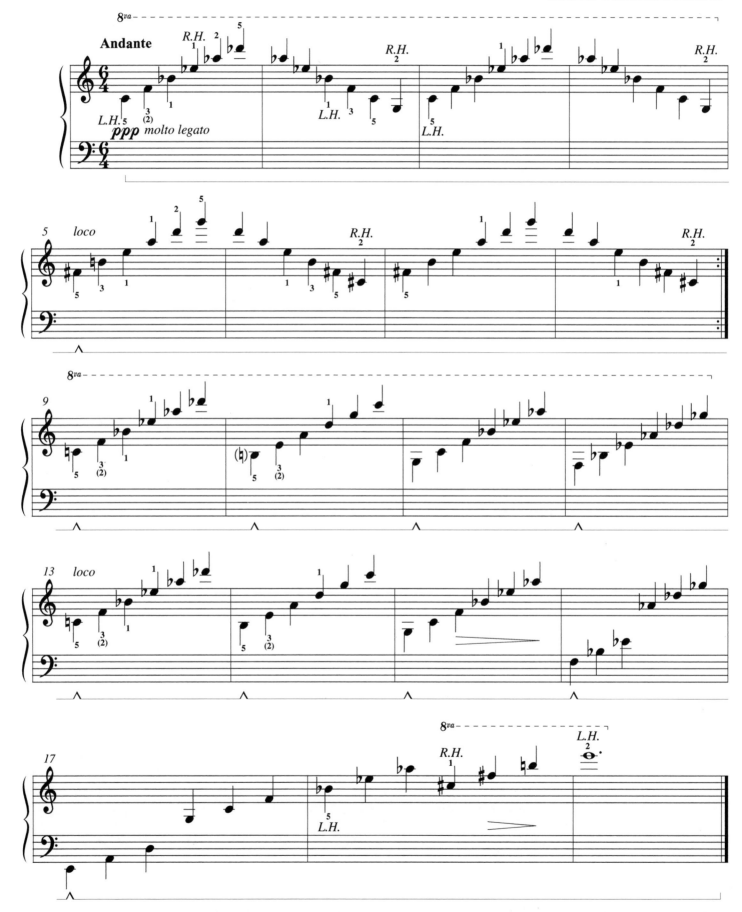

for Georgia Katherine Bowder-Newton

Pedaling Along

Op. 108, No. 11

Dianne Goolkasian Rahbee

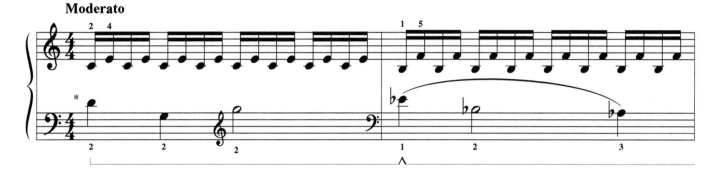

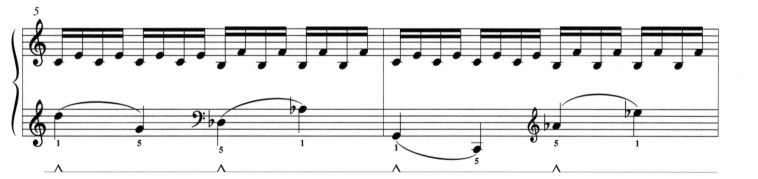

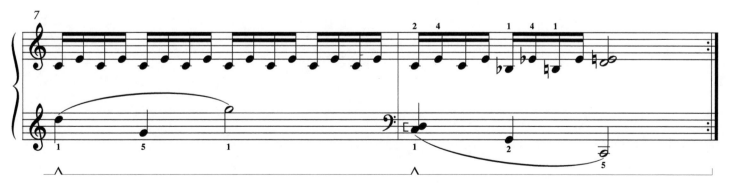

* Lift finger high off of each note and let the pedal connect the tones.

Essay

Dianne Goolkasian Rahbee

This piece is a staccato study in seconds.

March tempo

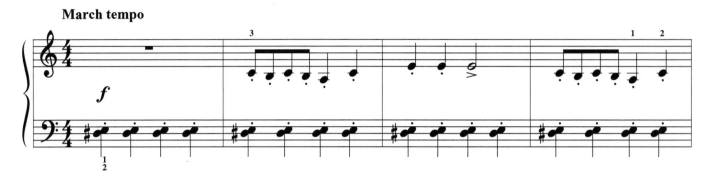

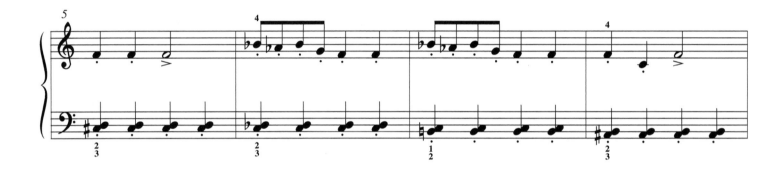

Impatience

from Expressions

Op. 8, No. 1

Dianne Goolkasian Rahbee

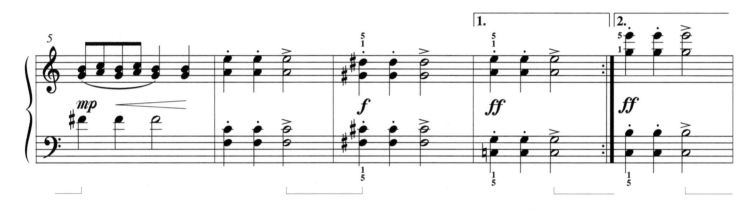

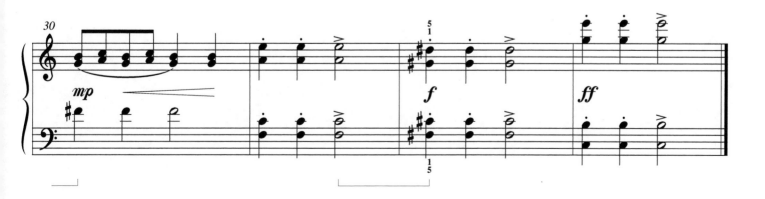

Etude in C

from Expressions

Op. 8, No. 7

Dianne Goolkasian Rahbee

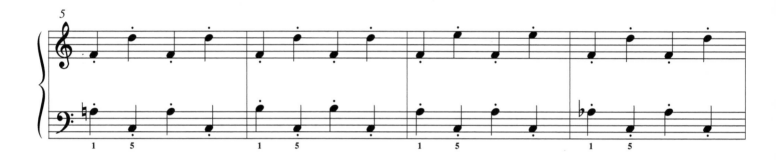

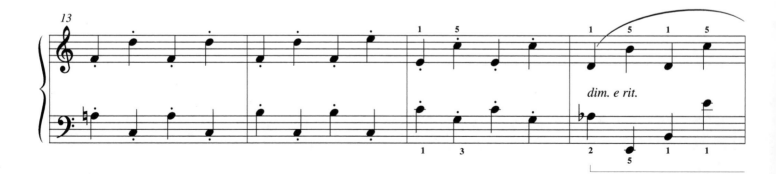

Andante - Molto rubato

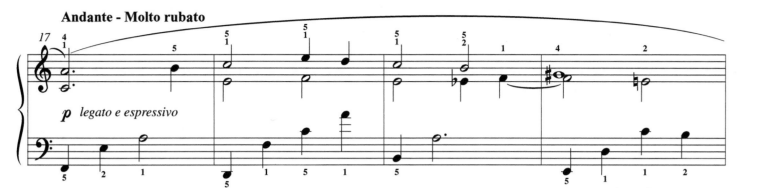

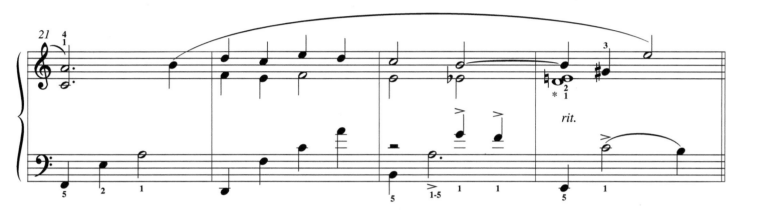

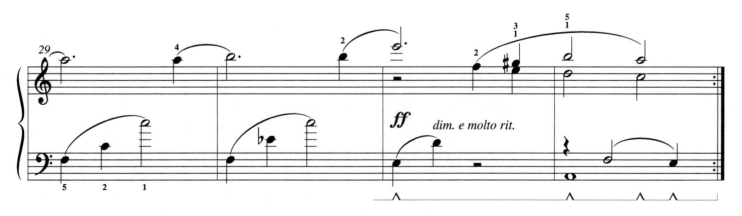

* Editor's note: for a smaller hand, lift the fingers off of the whole notes in order to play the upper melodic notes.

for Aaron Whiting Schmitt

Fanfare No. 7

Op. 110, No. 7

Dianne Goolkasian Rahbee

Moderato, like heralding trumpets

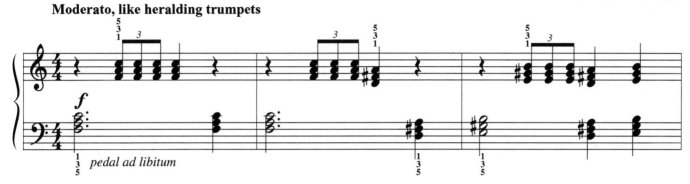

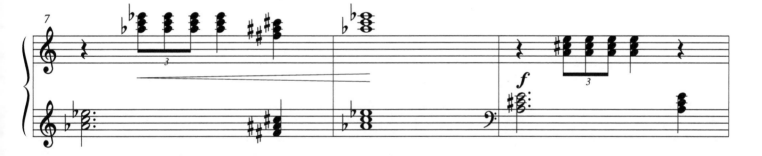

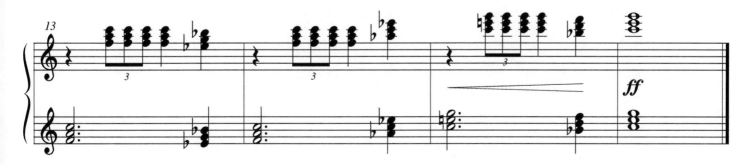

Harlequin Waltz

from Expressions

Op. 8, No. 8

Dianne Goolkasian Rahbee

Moderato, molto rubato, with humor

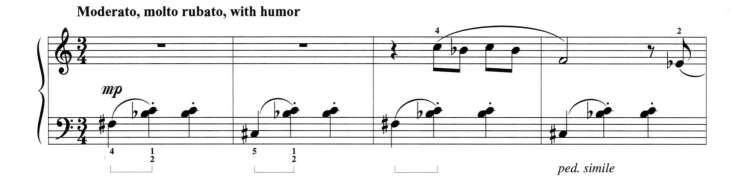

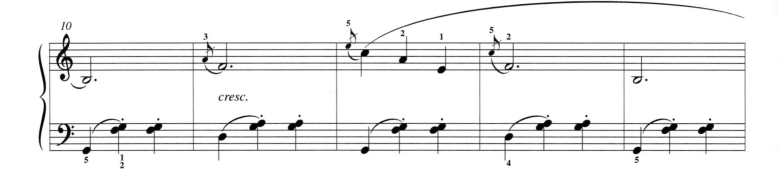

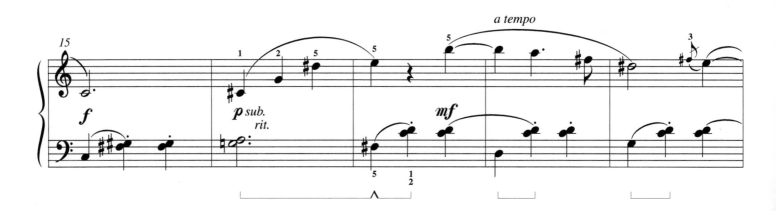

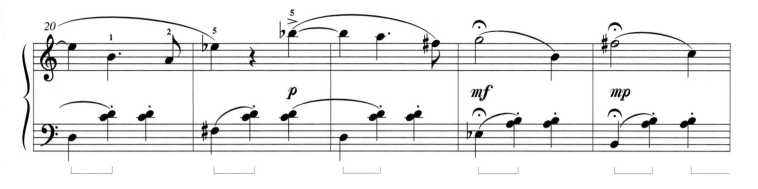

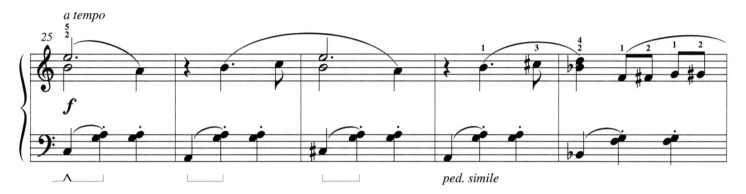

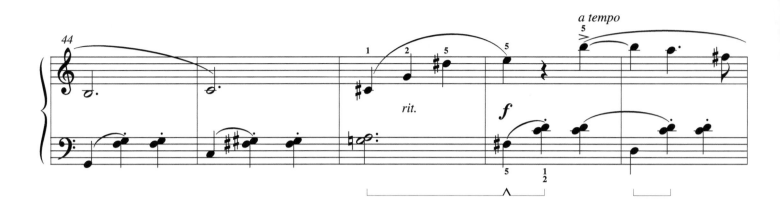

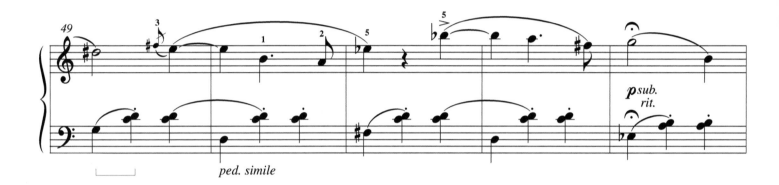

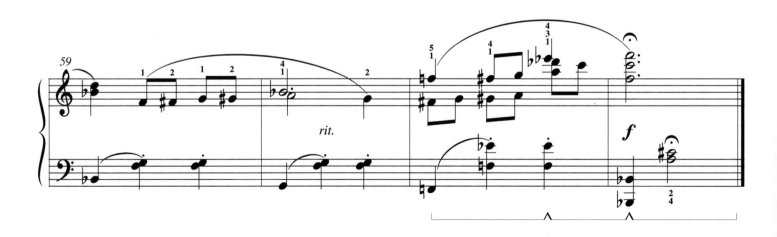

for Timothy Richard DerMarderosian

Fanfare No. 9

Op. 110, No. 9

Dianne Goolkasian Rahbee

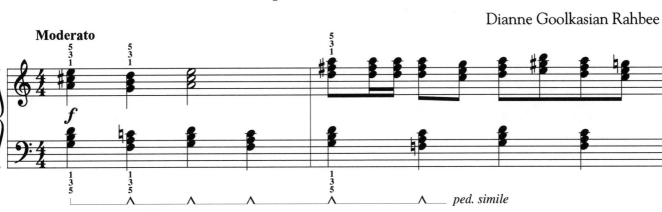

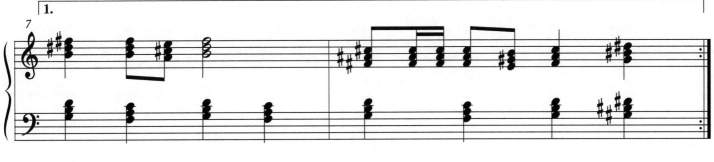

for Hope Kalajian

Popcorn Toccatina

Op. 108, No. 10

Dianne Goolkasian Rahbee

Popping briskly!

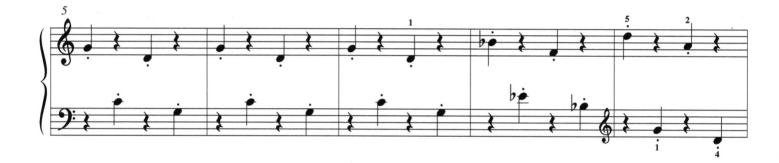

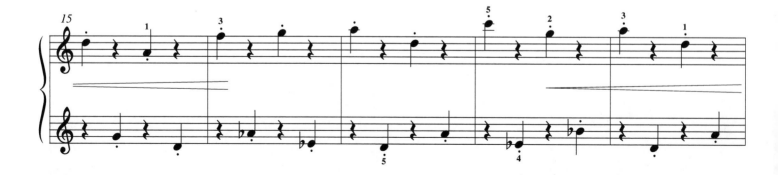

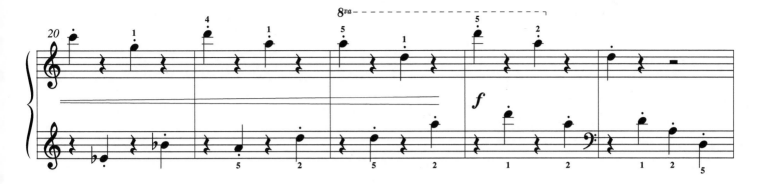

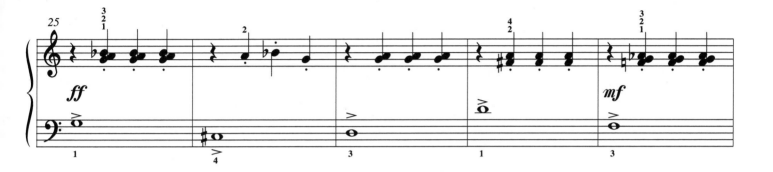

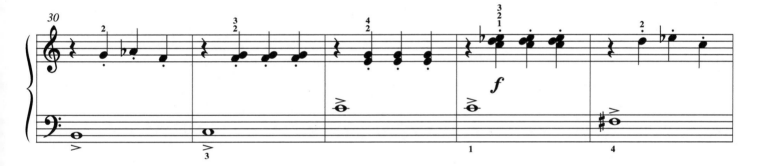

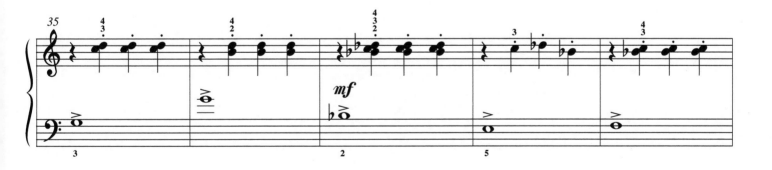

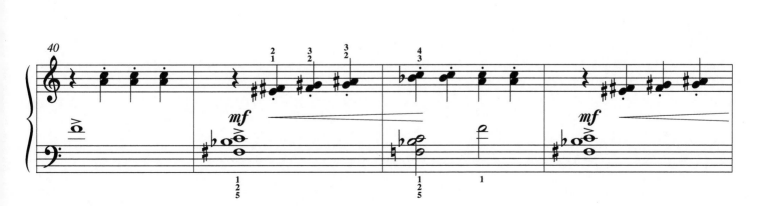

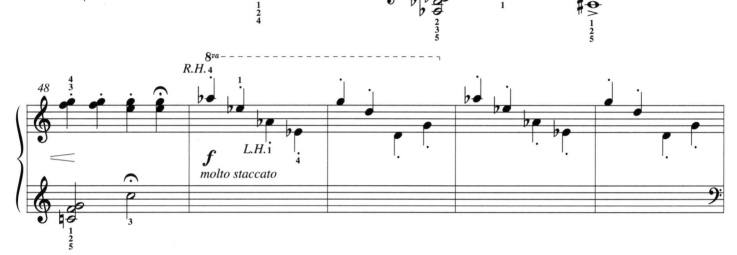

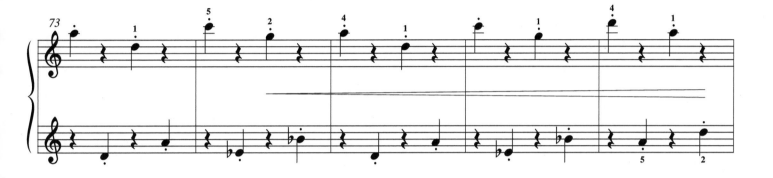

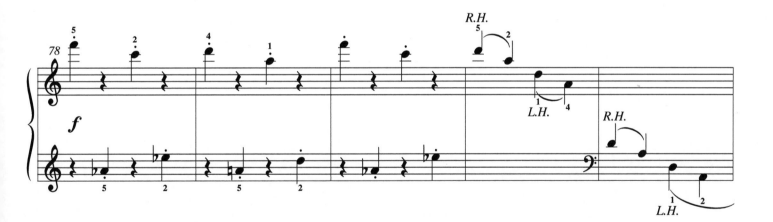

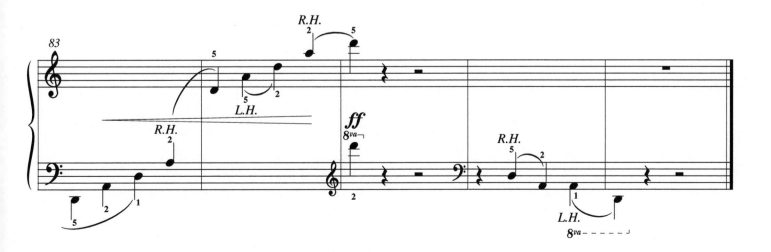

for Edward (Ted) Hennessy (1966-2001)

Prelude

In Memoriam
Op. 116

Dianne Goolkasian Rahbee

With feelings of anguish after the World Trade Center disaster 9/11/01.

Molto espressivo (♩ = ca. 92)

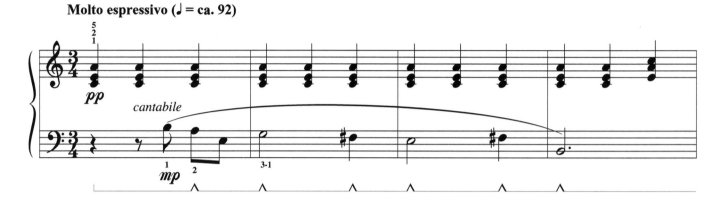

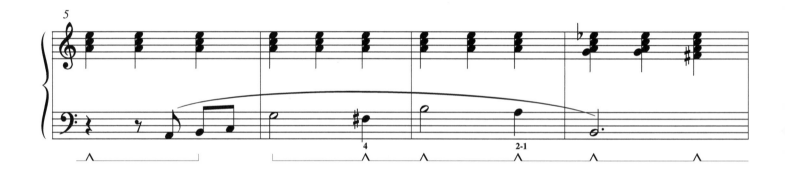

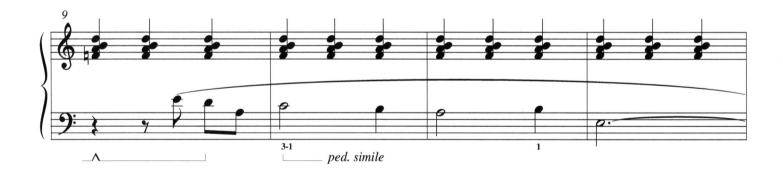

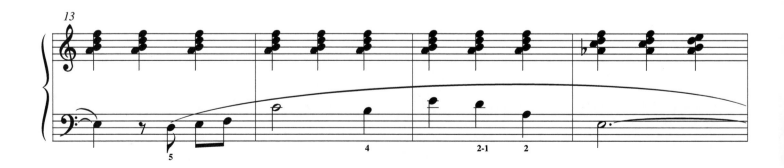

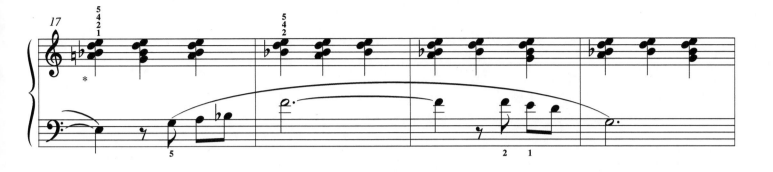

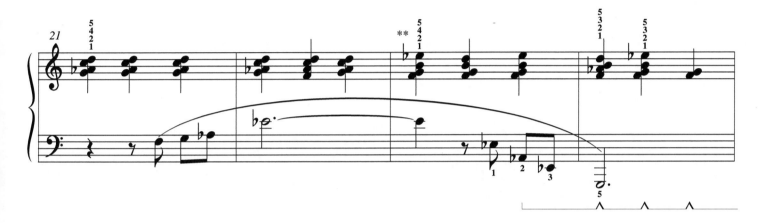

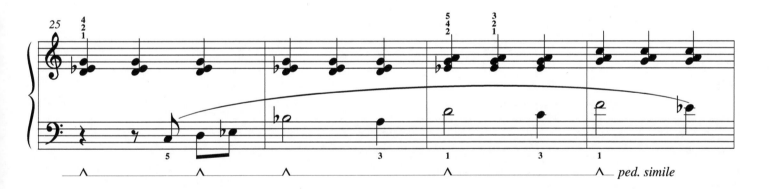

* Bring out the bottom voice of the R.H. chords.
**Bring out the top notes of the R.H. chords.

Dancing Puppet

from Expressions

Op. 8, No. 9

Dianne Goolkasian Rahbee

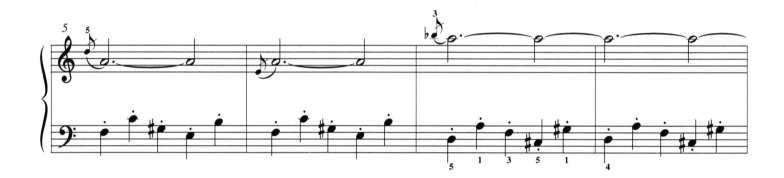

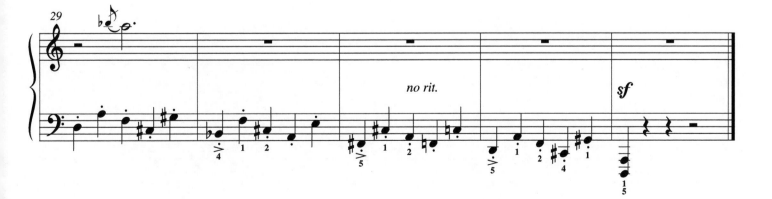

for Benedek Horvath

March

Op. 105, No. 1

Dianne Goolkasian Rahbee

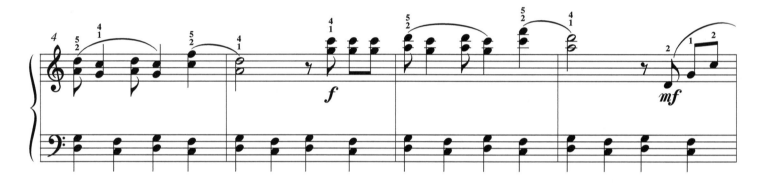

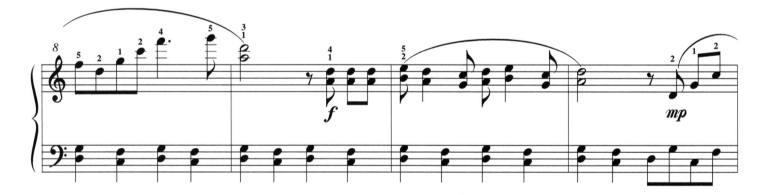

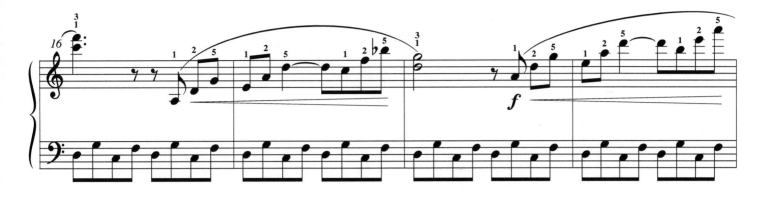

for Marteen Van Kerckhoven

Peaceful Child

Op. 105, No. 2

Dianne Goolkasian Rahbee

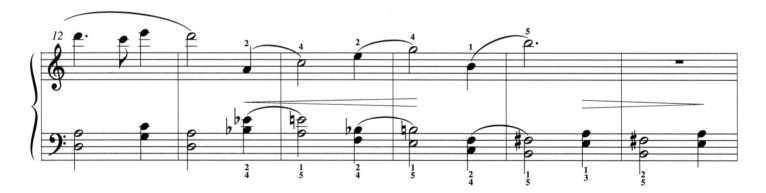

J1011

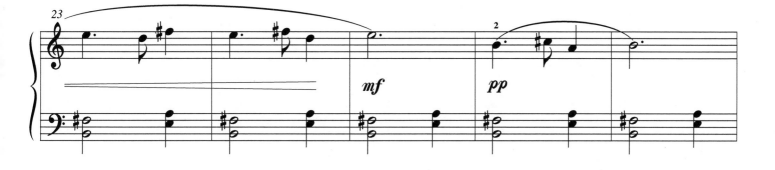

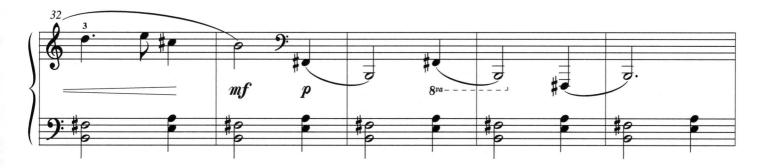

for Benedek Horvath

Forward March

Op. 105, No. 5

Dianne Goolkasian Rahbee

for Alexander Joseph Guertin

Sequence Etude

Op. 110, No. 4

Dianne Goolkasian Rahbee

Look for repeating fingering and note patterns and for descending L.H. perfect fifth patterns.

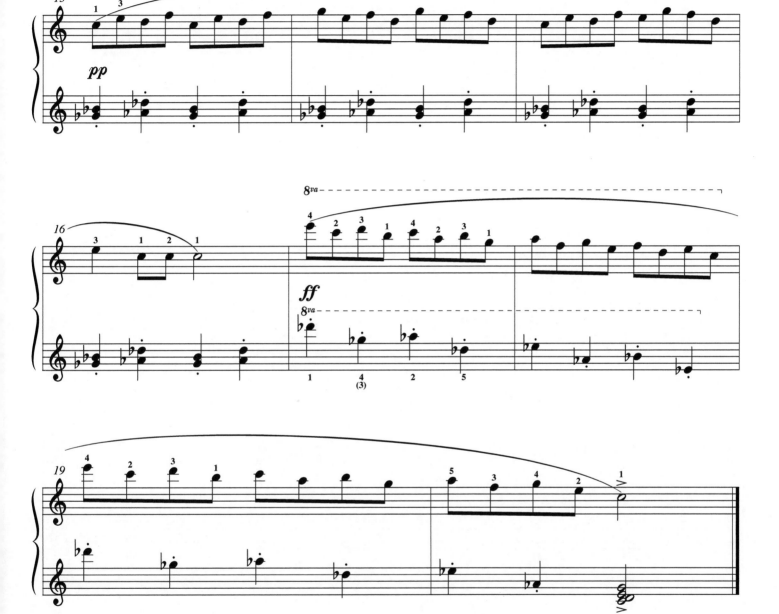

Perfect Fifth Etude

from Three Little Interval Etudes

Dianne Goolkasian Rahbee

Glissando Etude

Op. 74, No. 2

Dianne Goolkasian Rahbee

Play evenly so that the piece sounds like a series of glissandi.

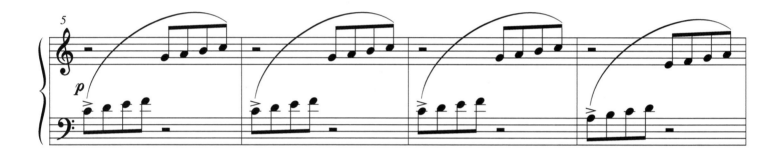

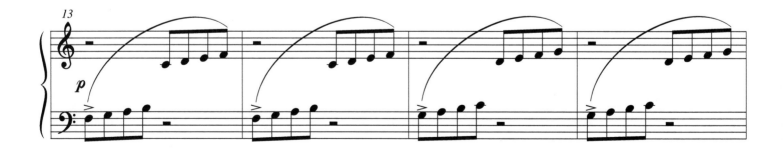

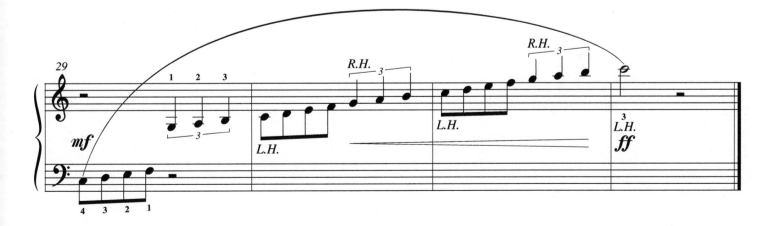

Major Third Etude

from Three Little Interval Etudes

Dianne Goolkasian Rahbee

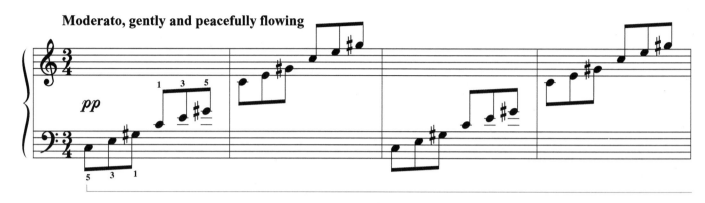

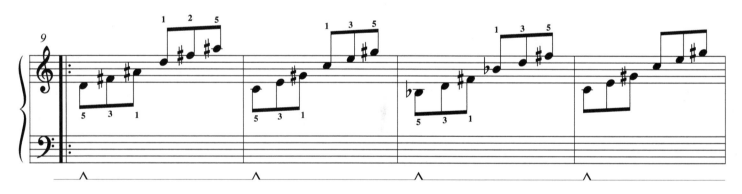

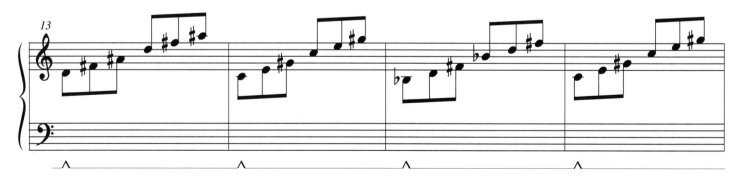

*Although the eighth notes are divided in groups of three because the hands are divided accordingly, the musical sense should be felt in ¾ and not ⁶⁄₈ time. It could be played either way, but the musical sense is altogether different. Try playing it both ways and see the difference.

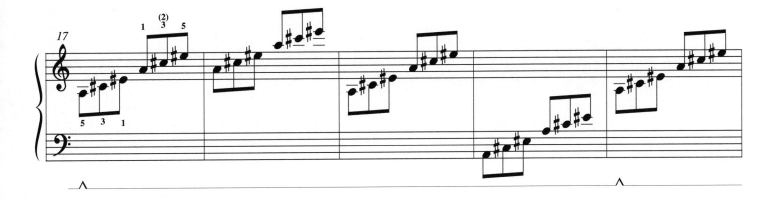

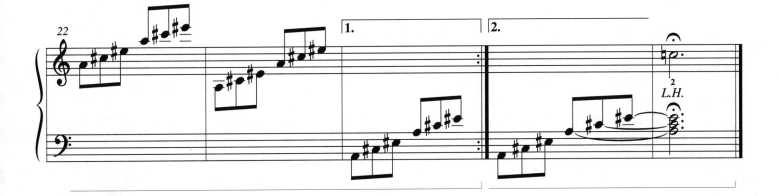

Minor Second Etude

from Three Little Interval Etudes

Dianne Goolkasian Rahbee

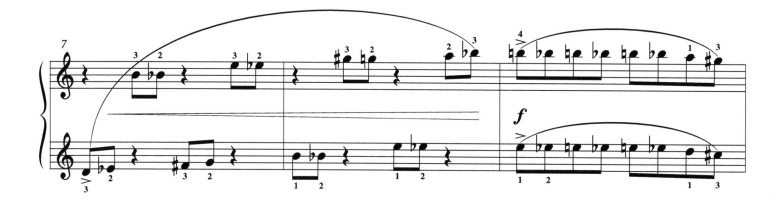

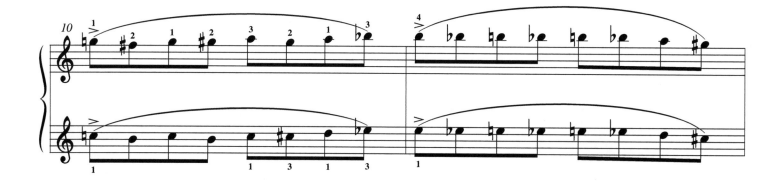

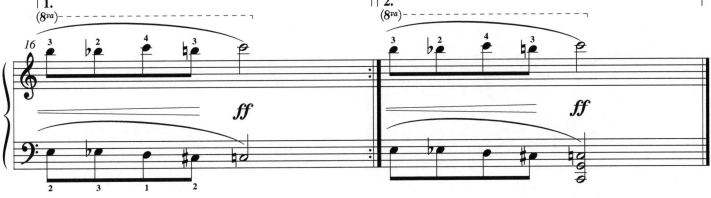

Fourth Interval Etude

Op. 74, No. 4

Bring out the top notes of the intervals of a 4th in the R.H.,
and use a flexible wrist and arm to shape the phrases.

Dianne Goolkasian Rahbee

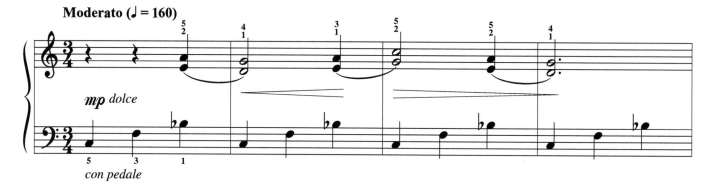

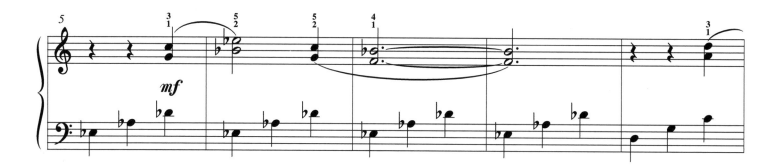

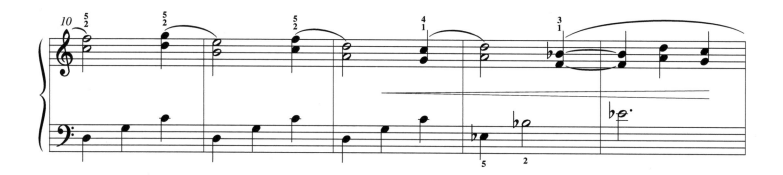

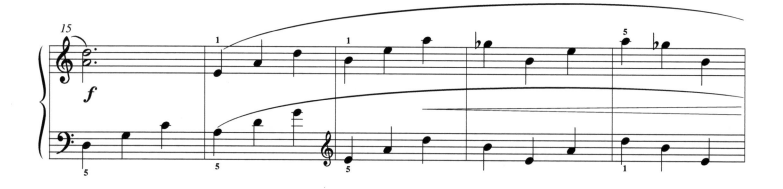

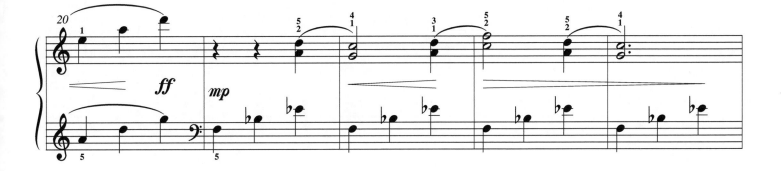

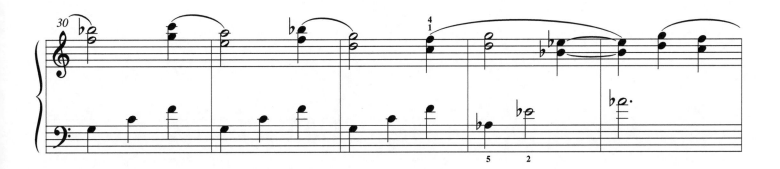

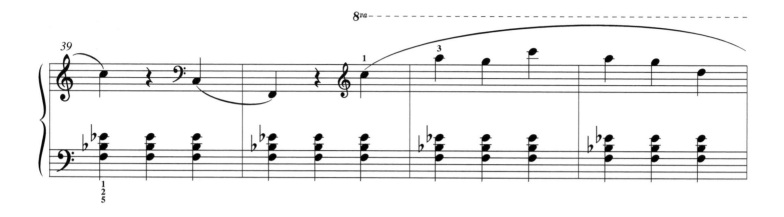

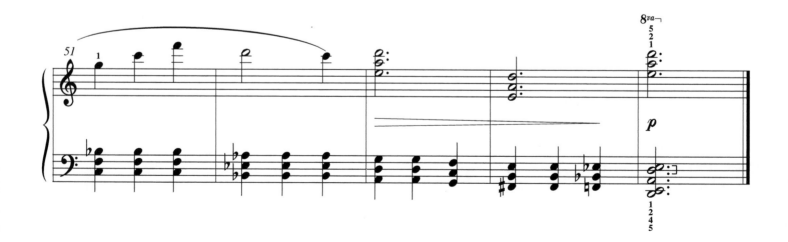

Parallel Sixth Etude

Op. 74, No. 1

Balance the right hand chords so that the top note of each chord sings out.
Be sure to use a loose wrist.

Dianne Goolkasian Rahbee

As fast as possible

Two options:

1) Play the R.H. part filling in with first inversion triads using the 2nd finger.

2) Try playing the piece through using each of the L.H. rhythms below.

Parallel Third Etude

Op. 74, No. 3

Dianne Goolkasian Rahbee

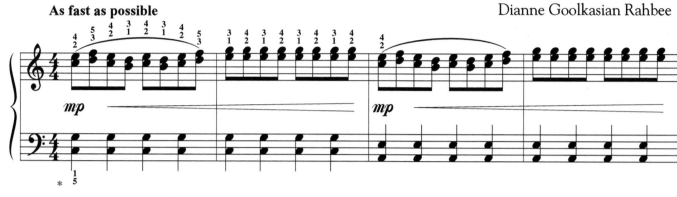

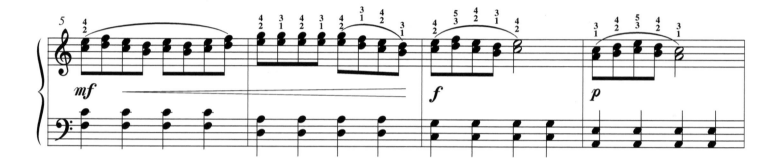

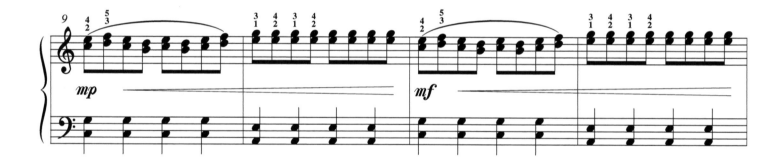

* The R.H. may also be played with only fingers (4-2) throughout the entire piece.

Optional L.H. accompaniment patterns: Try playing the piece using each of the rhythms below.

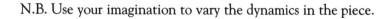

N.B. Use your imagination to vary the dynamics in the piece.

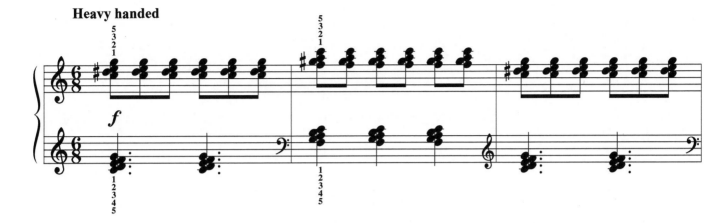

for Alexander Deron Torcomian

Blustering Clusters

Cluster Etude
Op. 108, No. 9

Dianne Goolkasian Rahbee

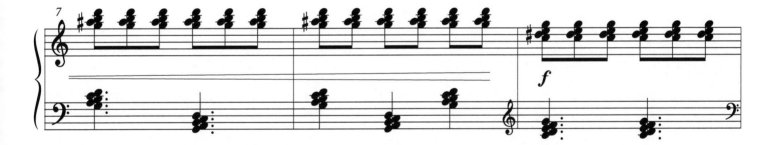

J1011

$\frac{5}{4}$ Time Etude

Op. 74, No. 5

Dianne Goolkasian Rahbee

Moderato (♩ = 200)

* You can design your own dynamics for the piece.

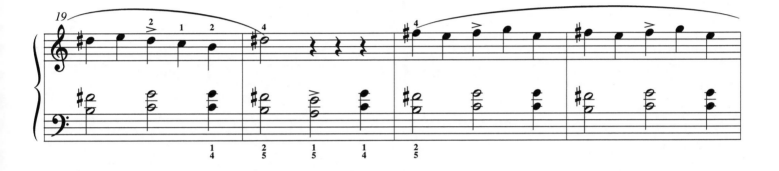

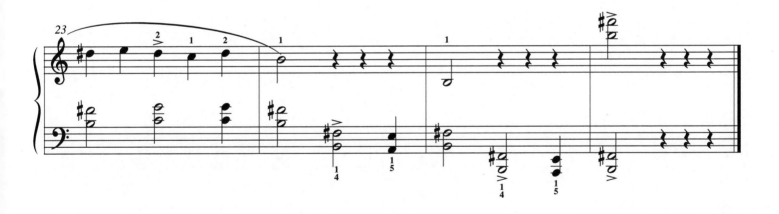

Jumping Sfz Etude

Op. 74, No. 7

Dianne Goolkasian Rahbee

As fast as possible, full of lively energy!

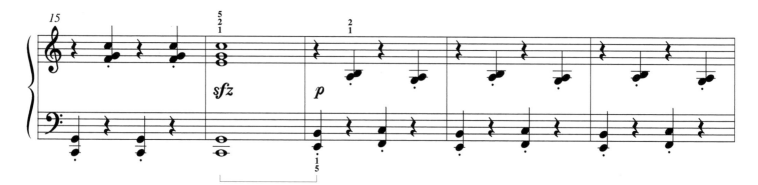

* Keep the same fingering throughout except where indicated.

for Benedek Horvath

Here and There

Op. 105, No. 6

Dianne Goolkasian Rahbee

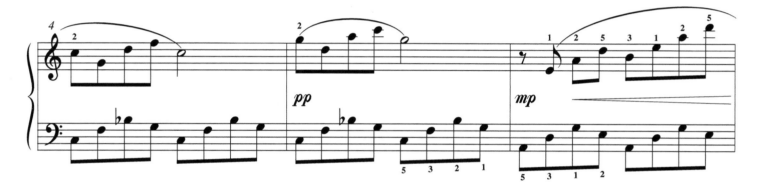

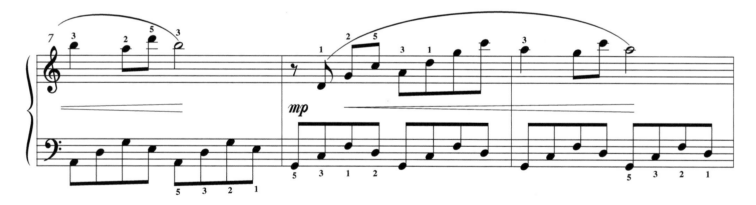

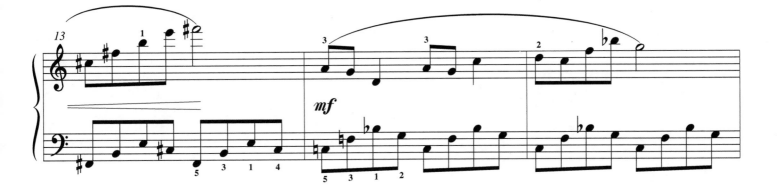

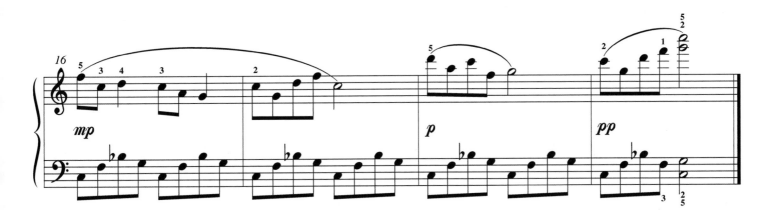

Pedal Etude

Op. 74, No. 6

Chords built in perfect 4ths are used a great deal in modern music.
It is important to become comfortable with this unusual hand position and sound.

Dianne Goolkasian Rahbee

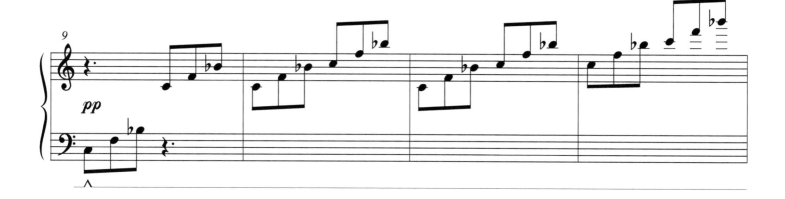

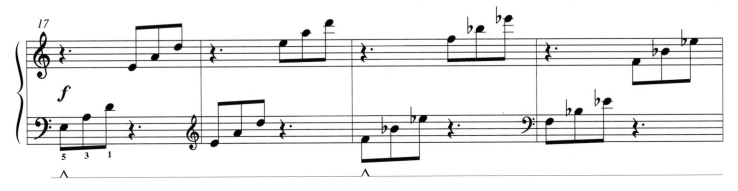

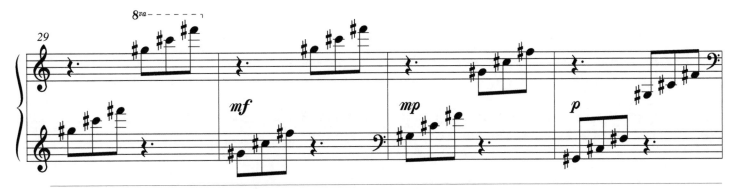

This piece was commissioned by the New Jersey Chapter of MTNA in 2003

Adventurous Journey
Op. 133

Dianne Goolkasian Rahbee

Allegretto scherzando

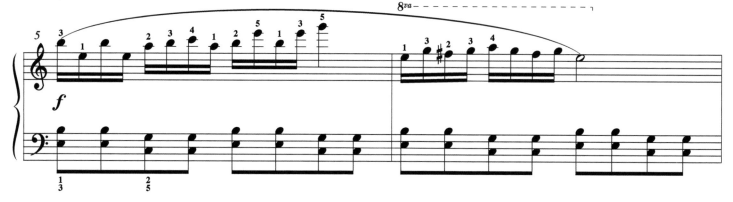

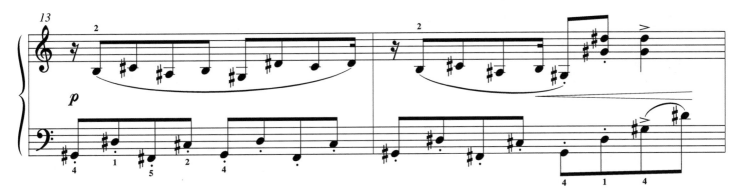

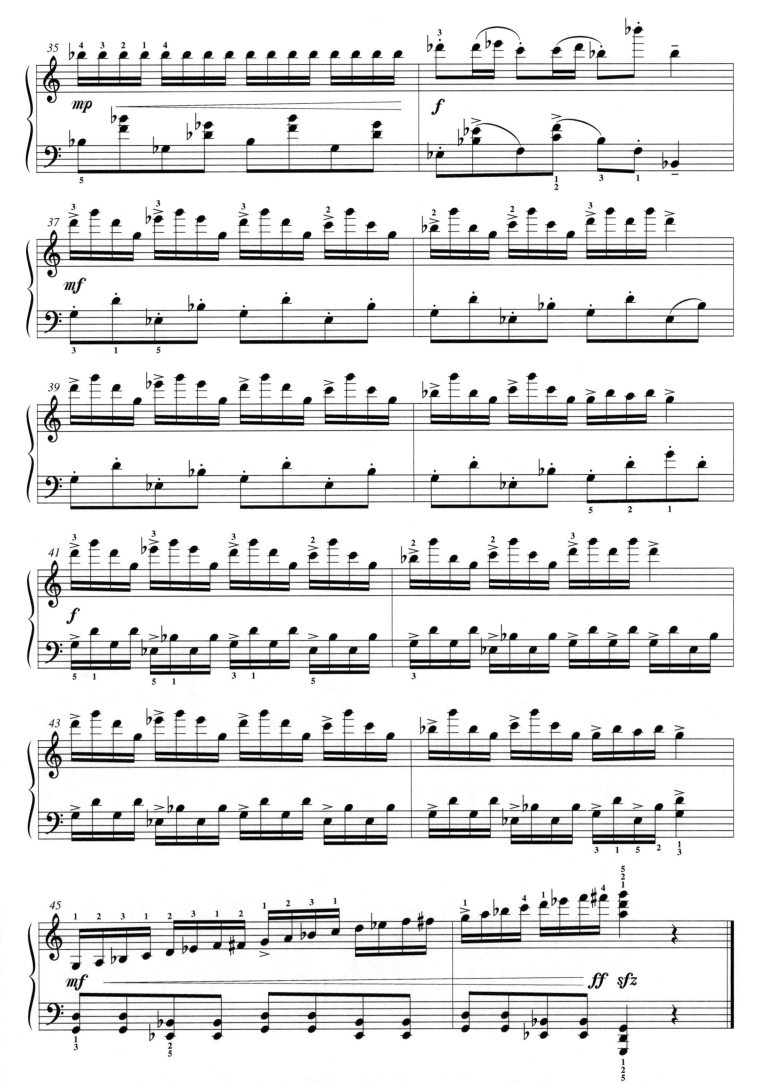

for Benedek Horvath

Running Around

Op. 105, No. 4

Dianne Goolkasian Rahbee

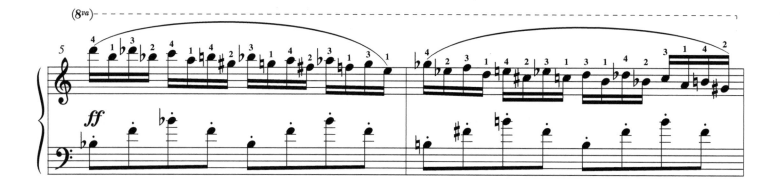

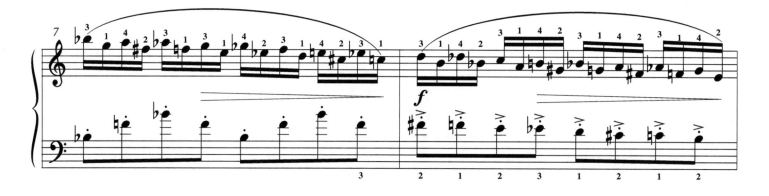

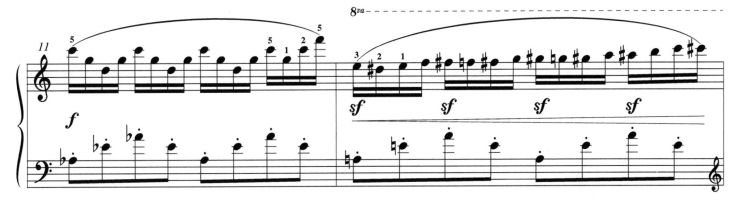

This piece was commissioned by the New Jersey Chapter of MTNA in 2003

Monday Morning in the City

Dianne Goolkasian Rahbee

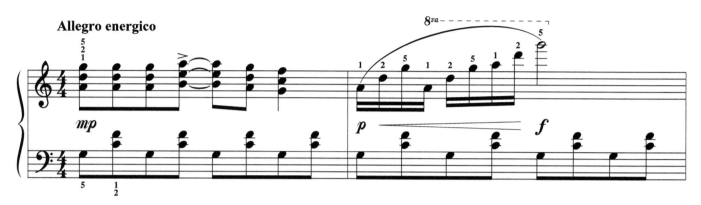

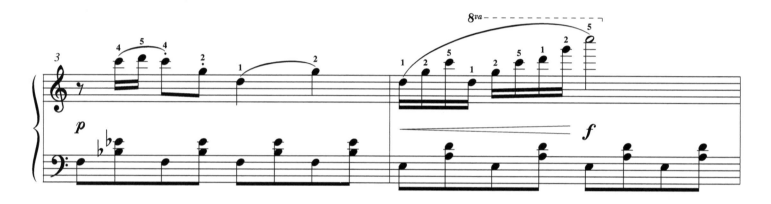

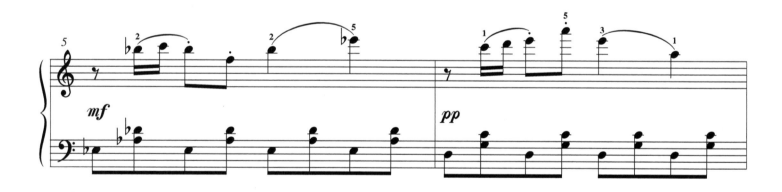

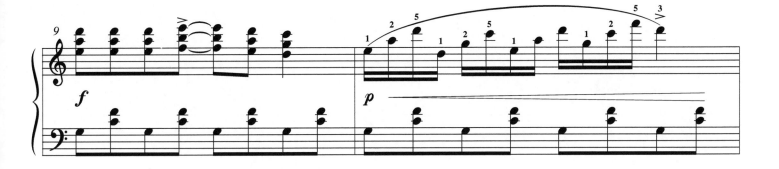

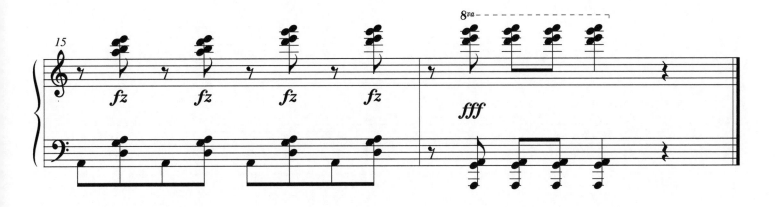

for Teddy Hennessy

Toccatina No. 1

from Five Toccatinas

Dianne Goolkasian Rahbee

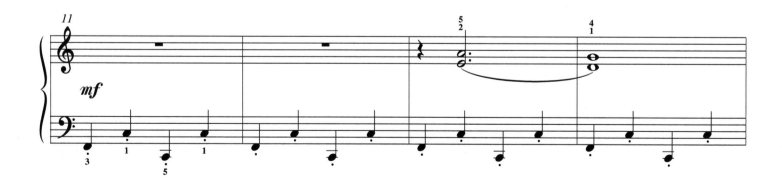

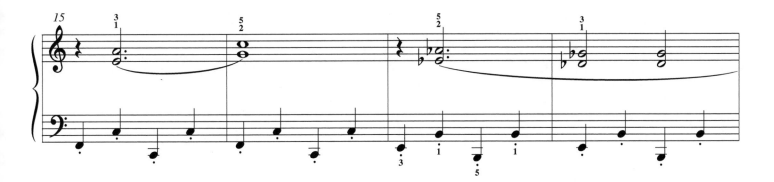

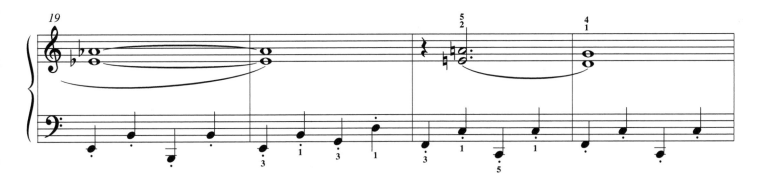

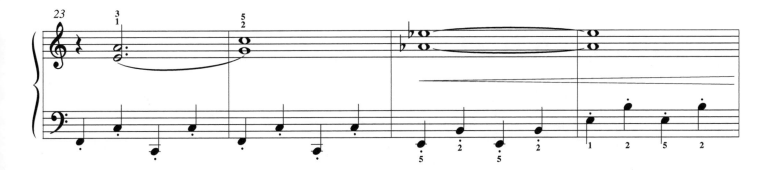

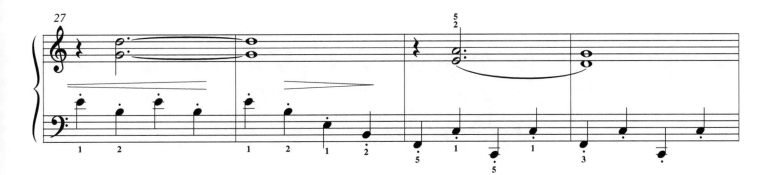

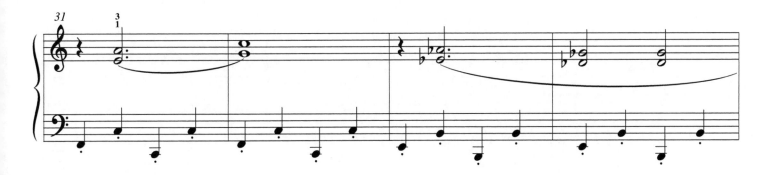

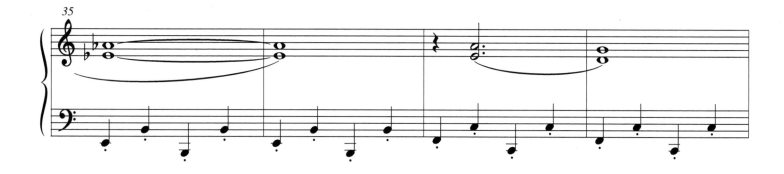

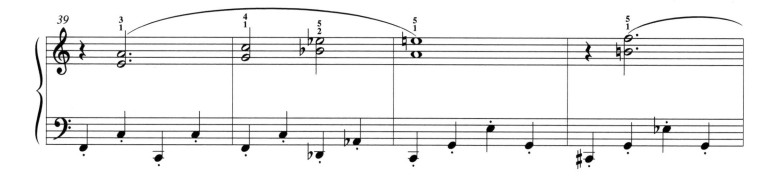

for Nicole Nelson

Toccatina No. 2

from Five Toccatinas

Dianne Goolkasian Rahbee

Allegretto (♩ = 120)

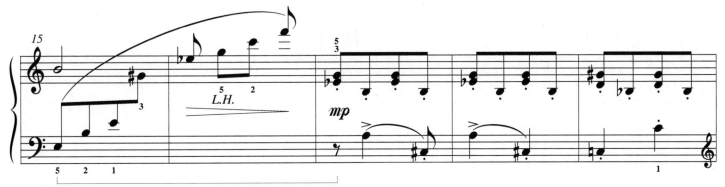

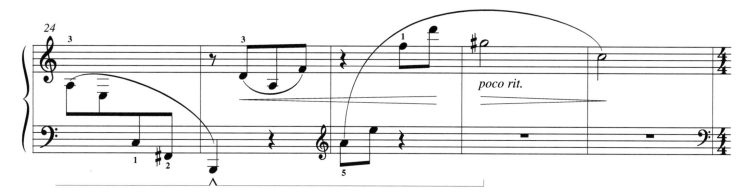

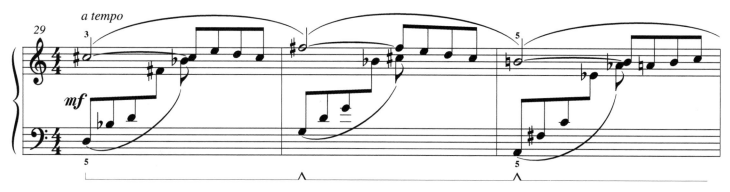

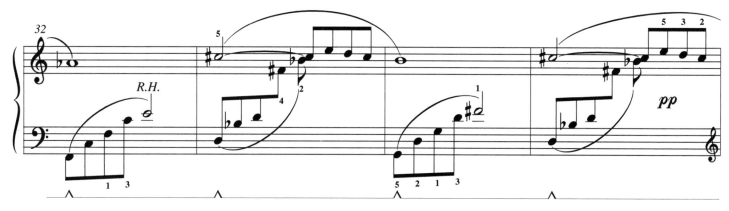

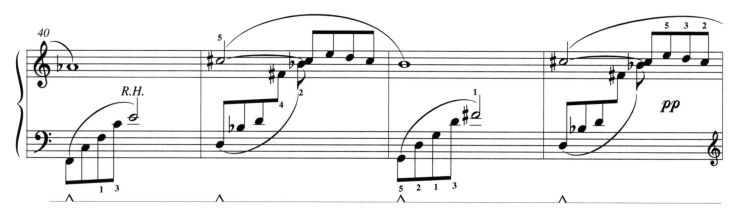

for Antoine Louis Moeldner

Toccatina No. 3

from Five Toccatinas

Dianne Goolkasian Rahbee

Allegretto (♩ = 120)

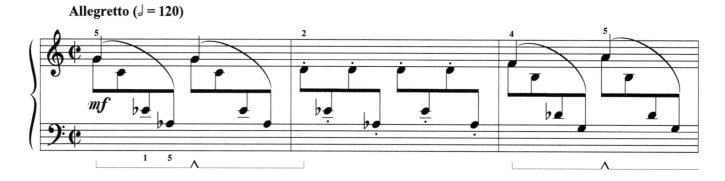

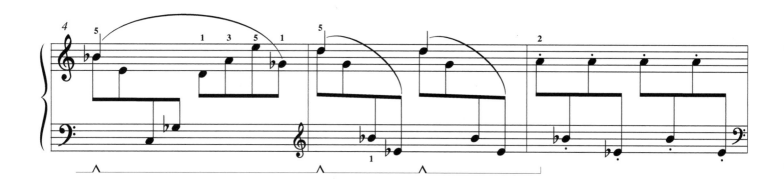

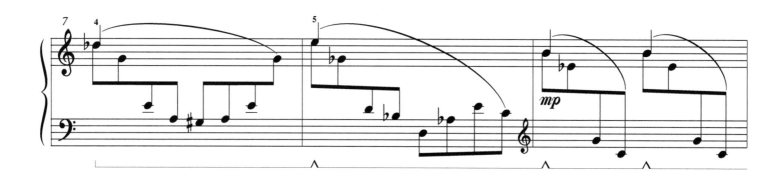

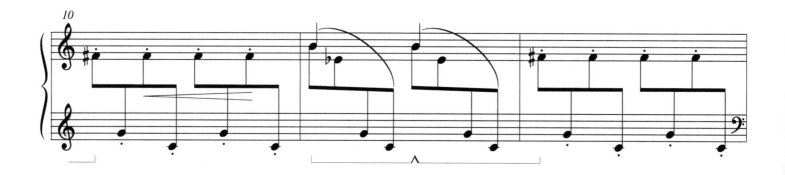

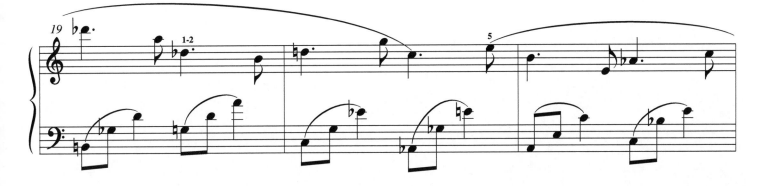

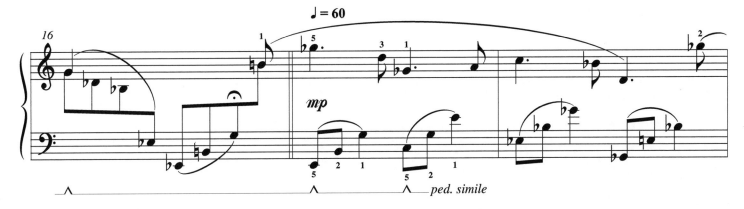

Tempo I

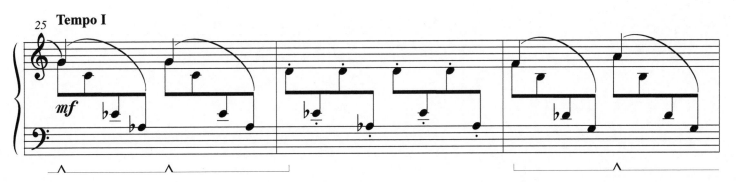

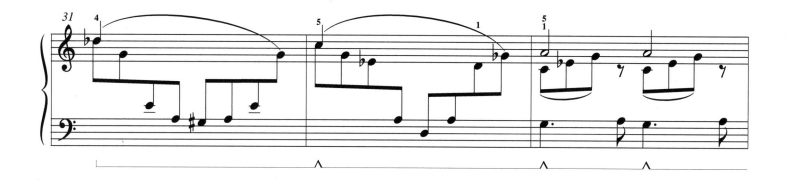

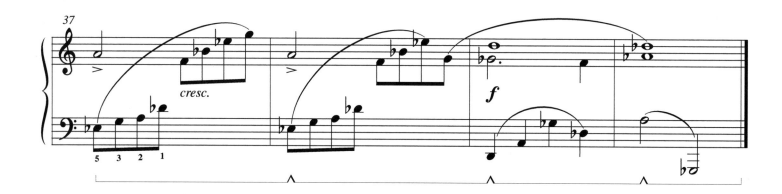

for Erika Kuno

Toccatina No. 4

from Five Toccatinas

Dianne Goolkasian Rahbee

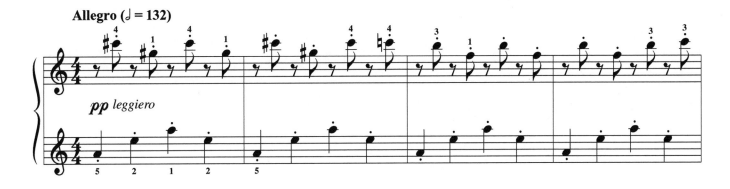

J1011

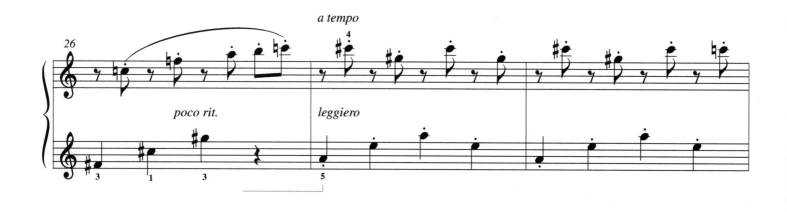

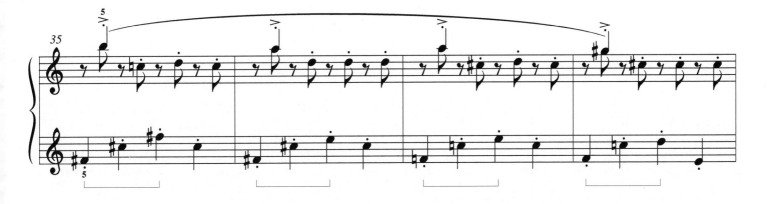

for Alisa Kuno

Toccatina No. 5

from Five Toccatinas

Dianne Goolkasian Rahbee

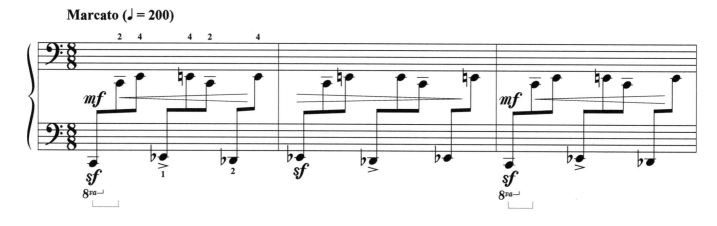

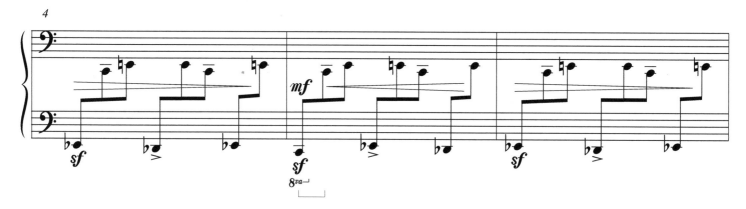

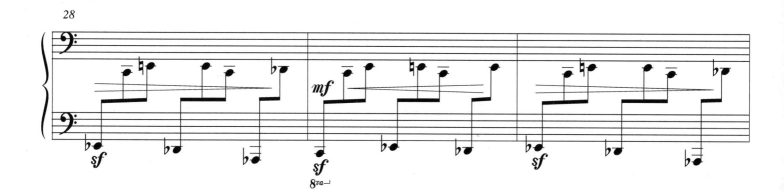

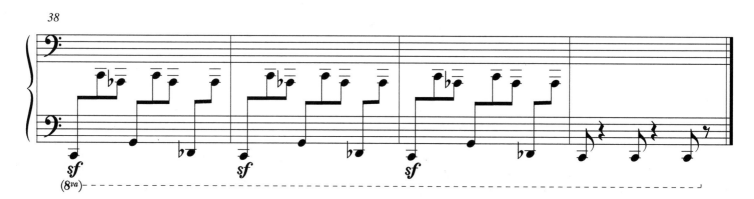

* The 8va beginning in measure 33 applies to the L.H. only.